Baby Coming

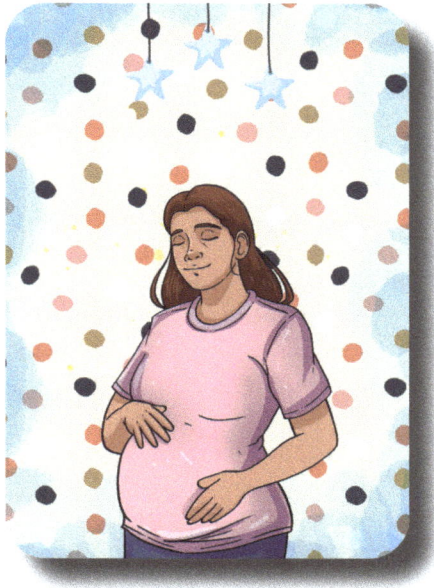

By Craig Williams

Library For All Ltd.

Baby Coming

First published 2023

Published by Library For All Ltd
Email: info@libraryforall.org
URL: libraryforall.org

Our Yarning logo design by Jason Lee, Bidjipidji Art

Original illustrations by John Robert Azuelo

Baby Coming
Williams, Craig
ISBN: 978-1-923110-00-7
SKU03349

Baby Coming

Kali and Jordon were going to have a baby really soon.

As they went to visit Dad Craig one sunny day, Kali had a big shock when her water broke.

Everyone was surprised and quickly started calling out what they should do. They called the hospital and grabbed the overnight bag.

Dad Craig said, "Get in the car, quick!"

Jordon helped Kali in the back. Her pains were coming fast.

They drove down the street towards the hospital, but next thing there was a big BANG! The car broke down right in the middle of the street.

Dad Craig called his son Tre, who lived close by. He came quickly to drive everyone to the hospital safely.

Kali was being tough, but her pains were getting worse, and she was worried her baby might be born in the car.

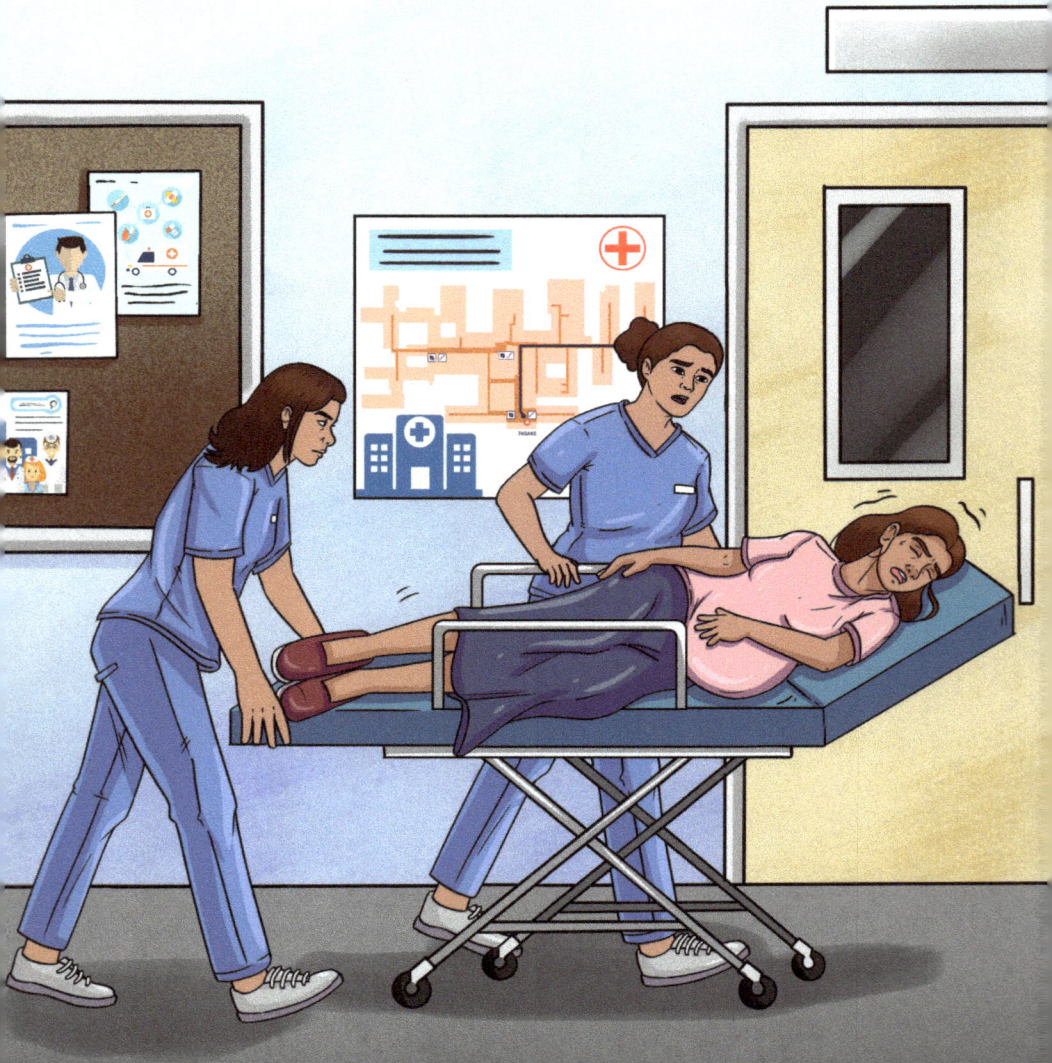

They all arrived at the hospital and the nurses helped Kali to the delivery room.

After a wait, baby Eliza was born, and everyone cheered. What an adventure for the family!

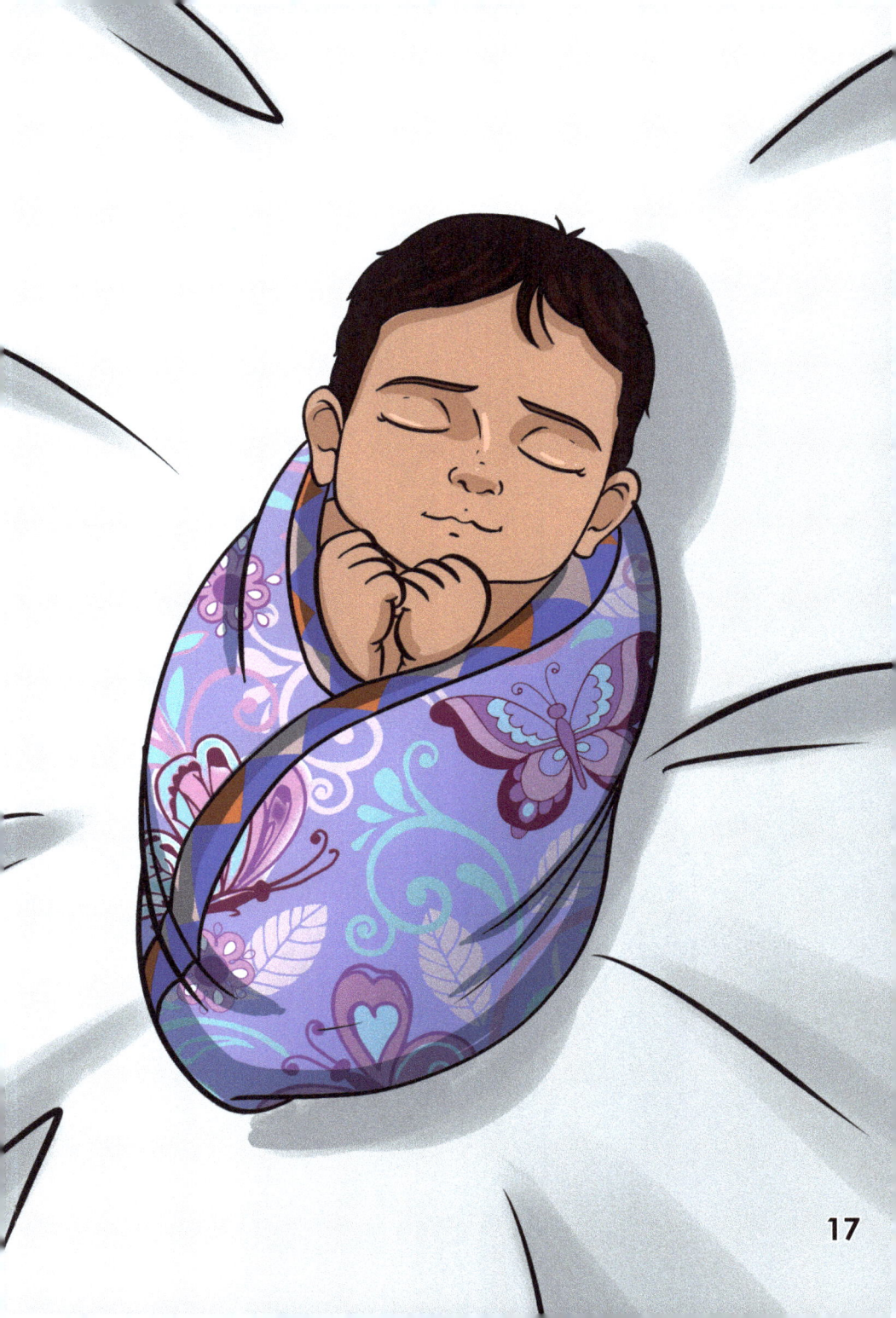

Dad Craig was a proud new Pop and he drove Jordan, Kali, and baby Eliza home to meet the rest of the family.

You can use these questions to talk about this book with your family, friends and teachers.

What did you learn from this book?

Describe this book in one word. Funny? Scary? Colourful? Interesting?

How did this book make you feel when you finished reading it?

What was your favourite part of this book?

download our reader app
getlibraryforall.org

About the author

Craig was born in Narrandera from the Wiradjuri Nation and lives in Queanbeyan. He loves sharing stories with family.

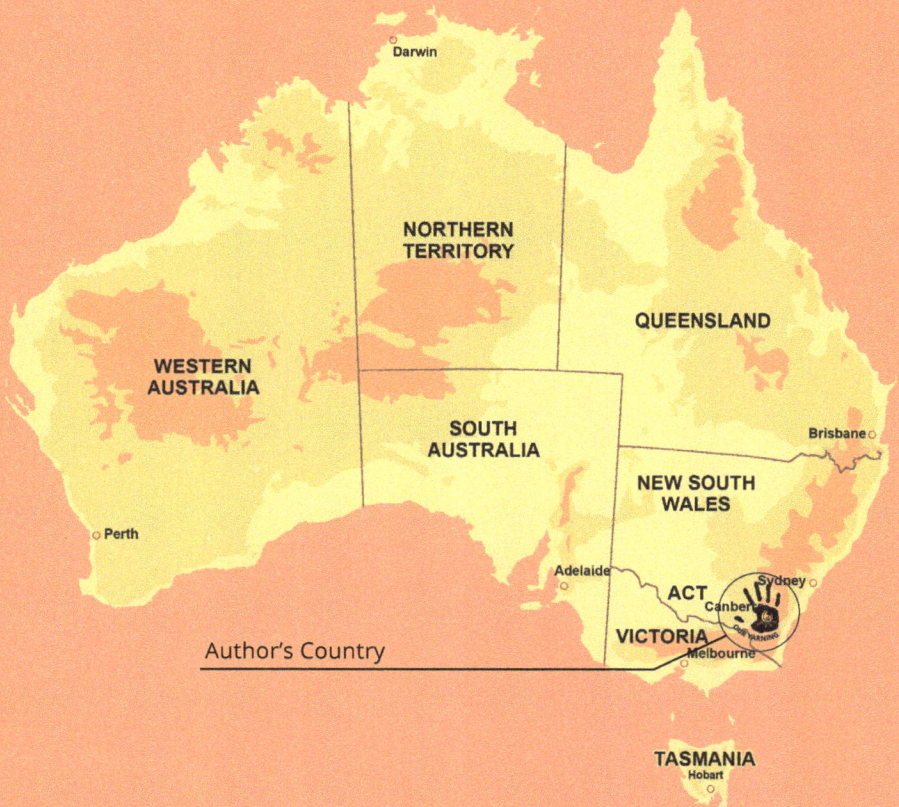

Darwin

NORTHERN
TERRITORY

QUEENSLAND

WESTERN
AUSTRALIA

SOUTH
AUSTRALIA

Brisbane

NEW SOUTH
WALES

Perth

Adelaide

Sydney

ACT
Canberra

Author's Country

VICTORIA
Melbourne

TASMANIA
Hobart

Our Yarning

Want to discover more books from this collection? Our Yarning is a collection of books written by Aboriginal and Torres Strait Islander peoples across Australia.

We know that children learn better, and enjoy reading more, when they see themselves in the stories, characters and illustrations of the books they read.

To download the app, visit the Google Play Store on any Android device and search 'Our Yarning'.

libraryforall.org

www.ingramcontent.com/pod-product-compliance
Lightning Source LLC
Chambersburg PA
CBHW042346040426
42448CB00019B/3421